young PIONEERS

By Tisha Hamilton

Modern Curriculum Press
Parsippany, New Jersey

Credits

Photos: Wraparound cover: Montana Historical Society, Helena. Title page: The Kansas State Historical Society, Topeka, Kansas. 5: Courtesy of Union Pacific Railroad Museum. 9: Henry E. Huntington Library and Art Gallery. 12: WY Recreation Commission. 13: N. Carter/North Wind Picture Archives. 14: Corbis/Bettmann. 16–17: Used by permission, Utah State Historical Society, all rights reserved, Photo no. 477. 19: James L. Amos/Corbis. 20: The Corcoran Gallery of Art. 22: Nebraska State Historical Society. 23: Corbis/Bettmann. 25: Library of Congress. 26: Smithsonian Institution. 27: Library of Congress. 28: Ewing Galloway. 31: Culver Pictures. 32: ©Photo Researchers, Inc. 33: Chicago Historical Society. 34, 35: Nebraska State Historical Society. 36: Baldwin H. Ward/Corbis. 37: Corbis/Bettmann. 38–39: Solomon D. Butcher Collection/Nebraska State Historical Society. 40–41: Denver Public Library Western History Department. 42: Nebraska State Historical Society. 43: Annie Griffiths Belt/Corbis. 44: The Kansas State Historical Society, Topeka, Kansas. 45: Denver Public Library Western History Department. 46: Idaho State Historical Society. 47: Smithsonian Institution.
Illustrations: 6–7, 11: Steve Davies/Mapping Specialists.

Cover and book design by Lisa Ann Arcuri

ISBN 0-7652-2152-7

Printed in the United States of America
5 6 7 8 9 10 11   07 06 05 04 03

Modern
Curriculum
Press

Pearson Learning Group

1-800-321-3106
www.pearsonlearning.com

CONTENTS

For Bruce Coville, who showed me the way

1

WAGONS WEST

Can you imagine walking hundreds of miles across the United States? That's what the children of the pioneers did in the mid–1800s. That was when people started moving in long wagon trains from the eastern part of North America to the western part. In these trains, children mostly walked beside the wagons along with the adults.

A wagon train travels west.

In the 1830s, the United States was mostly a nation of farmers. Most Americans made their own clothes, grew their own food, and built their own homes. There were few factories or businesses in the southern states. Even in the northern states where there were cities like Boston and New York, there were not many big factories making goods and products.

In 1837, the country began having problems. The farmers had trouble with their crops and could not sell their corn and wheat. Bankers would not lend them any money. Families were hungry, and, unlike today, they could not go to the grocery store to buy what they needed.

In the 1840s, the United States greatly expanded its territory.

Oregon Territory
Claimed by England
until 1846

Missouri R.

Louisiana Purchase 1803

Utah Territory

Owned by Mexico until 1848

California

New Mexico Territory

Texas Became part of the U.S. in 1845

PACIFIC OCEAN

MEXICO

Also in the 1830s, most of the United States lay east of the Mississippi River. All the rest of the land that would become the United States today was still open territory. The farmers began to hear about land in the western part of this territory where they could take their families and start a new life. They heard that the land was free. Some people said there was gold to be found in the ground. All they had to do was go there and build a new home.

The first people to move from the East to the West called themselves emigrants because they were leaving the United States to travel to a new land. They later became known as pioneers because they were the first to do something.

A big part of the open land was prairie covered with tall, thick grass. Many people did not think this was a place where they wanted to live because there were so few trees and little rain. People knew the land in the far west was different. They had heard from others that it was rich and fertile.

Most news about the West came from people who had gotten a letter from relatives who had made the journey, or people who had heard from others about pioneers who had gone west. Some people who had made the trip wrote guidebooks that were sold in the East. These books tried to convince people to head west.

Not all of the guidebooks were truthful about what new settlers would find in the West. The guidebooks usually told only about the good things, such as the beautiful land, the rich soil, and the plentiful wildlife. They said little or nothing about the long stretches of trail with no water, how hard it was to cross the mountains, and the diseases that killed many pioneers.

Where the Mississippi River meets the Missouri River was the starting place for all the westward trails. The Missouri River was important because the pioneers could travel west by boat for many miles.

Rough frontier towns sprang up all along the river as more and more people headed west. These towns were known as the jumping-off places where the pioneers had to leave the boats and start traveling by wagon.

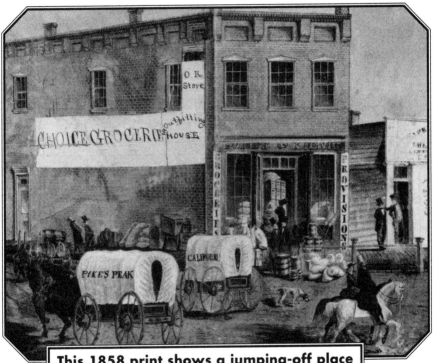

This 1858 print shows a jumping-off place on the Missouri River, one of the last places pioneers could buy supplies.

Families who wanted to go west usually would arrange to join a wagon train in one of these river towns. A wagon train was a group of wagons that traveled together in a long line. Some of the first wagon trains were big. One train had more than 1,000 people in hundreds of wagons. Many trains were smaller, with 35 to 50 wagons. In later years the wagon trains were much smaller. Sometimes just two or three wagons traveled together.

Timing was very important. Wagon trains left in late April or early May. If a family started out too early, the spring grasses would not have grown by the time they got to the prairie. This meant that the mules, oxen, horses, and other animals the pioneers brought with them would not be able to graze. Without fresh grass to eat, the animals would get sick or even die.

If a family started out too late, they might not reach the California or Oregon territories before winter came in October. They could get stuck in the western mountains, with fierce winter storms and deep snow swirling around them. Many families were stranded in this way. Some people died.

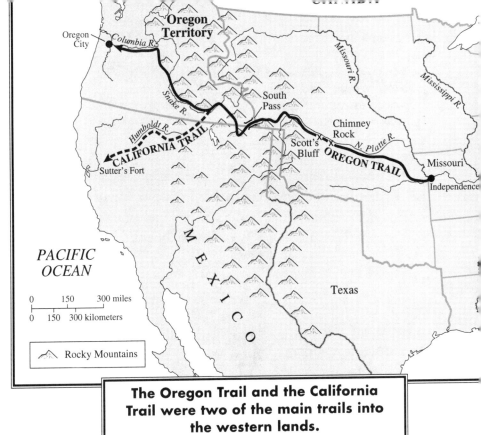

The Oregon Trail and the California Trail were two of the main trails into the western lands.

There were a number of trails the pioneers could take. Most people used the Oregon Trail, which was the best-known route. The trail ran for 2,400 miles over prairie grass, mountain rocks, and desert sand. After passing through the Rocky Mountains, the pioneers came to the halfway point. Here the trail divided. The northern part continued into Oregon. The southern part went into California.

Sometimes pioneers left signs for people who came after them. Many of these signs were warnings about bad water. Other signs marked places where people had died and were buried. Some signs pointed the way to routes that claimed to cut miles off the usual route. Many pioneers also carved their names and dates in rocks to show that they had gotten that far.

Most wagon trains had a captain, or someone to lead the way. Each family in the wagon train gave money to help pay the train captain. He would decide where to cross rivers, when to hurry, and where to stop.

No matter what route the pioneers chose, the trip took a long time. A wagon train usually had to travel four to five months to get to Oregon. The pioneers were willing to make the long trip. They wanted to get to the land they had been dreaming about so they could start a new life.

Old West Fact

In some places in Wyoming, you can still see the wagon wheel ruts worn in the ground by the pioneers' wagons.

Wagon wheel ruts worn into sandstone

MILES to Go

Before a family started west, they would buy a wagon, or they would fix their farm wagon. The pioneer wagons were called covered wagons because of the heavy cotton canvas that was stretched over bent wooden poles on the top.

The pioneers traveled in covered wagons.

A new wagon might have been painted bright blue, with a yellow front seat and bright red wheels. The canvas covering was clean and new. After a few weeks on the trail, the same wagon had chipped and peeling paint and mud splatters from one end to the other. Its canvas covering might have been torn. It was certainly worn and stained with dirt.

Yet this covered wagon was the closest thing to home that the pioneers would have on their journey. It was filled with clothing, furniture, tools, and supplies the pioneers needed to make the trip and to start their new homes in the West.

Most wagons were four feet wide and ten feet long. Packed inside there might have been a bed, a table and chairs, heavy wooden chests, and a china cupboard. There would probably have been a set of dishes, utensils, and pots and pans. There might have been large sacks of flour, sugar, potatoes, dried corn, bacon, and hard biscuits. There were also tools to fix a wagon wheel or anything else that might break. Tied to the outside of the wagon would have been a water barrel.

Along the trail the wagons sometimes got stuck in mud, or they had to be pulled up a steep mountainside or floated across a deep river. While crossing the desert, the animals sometimes became so weak from the dry, hot weather that they could no longer pull the heavy wagons. Then the pioneers had to take things out of their wagons and leave them on the trailside to lighten the load.

Deciding what they could get along without was based on what was needed to safely finish the journey. Tools and food were necessary. Heavy furniture and fancy china were not.

Everyone helped get a wagon out of the mud.

Many beautiful things were left behind on the western trail. Huge hand-carved tables sat by the side of the road, getting soaked by the rain and bleached by the sun. A china plate that may have belonged to someone's great-grandparents ended up in the dust. The pioneers may have been upset or sad about what they had to leave behind, but they had to keep going.

In a pioneer family the father probably drove the wagon. He would sit up front, holding the reins and guiding the horses, mules, or oxen that pulled the wagon.

The mother might sit on the front seat, holding a baby. Everyone else traveled on foot. Even boys and girls as young as five or six walked alongside the wagon.

A family might also have brought one or more cows so that they would have milk. There might have been chickens for eggs or even for a fried chicken dinner one night. There were often extra horses or oxen to lead. Some families even brought along pet cats and dogs.

Children may have helped by leading the larger farm animals, such as cows. They may have used a stick to keep the cows moving and in line. Other children may have carried a chicken or two in their arms.

Sometimes the pioneers were able to shoot birds, rabbits, a deer, or even a buffalo for fresh meat. Most of the time, however, they ate bacon every day, along with biscuits and beans.

Families tried to include vegetables in their meals, too. They might have been able to bring along a sack of potatoes or some dried corn. They also hoped to find plants that were good to eat along the way. Boys and girls would look for nuts, herbs, and other plants near the trail as they walked.

Butter was made while the wagons traveled. The pioneers would hang a covered pail of milk on the side of the wagon. As the wagon bumped and thumped along, the milk would slosh and churn. By the time the family stopped at the end of the day, the milk had turned into butter.

Butter bucket hooked to the back of a wagon

Old West Fact

One pioneer told of seeing ten tons of bacon alongside the trail. It had been left behind by others who could no longer carry it in their wagons because of the weight.

Chapter
3 Mud, Floods, and Buffalo Chips

Each long day of traveling began at sunrise. Long before then, while it was still dark, the pioneer family would begin to get ready for the day's journey. Children helped out in almost every way. One job was to get water in buckets made of wood or leather from a nearby river or other source of water.

The westward journey was a popular subject for some artists. This painting is by Benjamin Franklin Reinhart.

One bucket of water might have been used to wash hands and faces. Two or three buckets might have been used to water the animals. If the children were lucky, some water might have been saved to make hot oatmeal for breakfast. That didn't happen often. Usually in the morning the fires were put out, and there were only cold, dry biscuits for breakfast.

Some days the pioneers were able to make a short stop in the middle of the day to rest and eat. Sometimes they couldn't stop. They might have to hurry to get to the next stopping place before dark because that was the only place that had water.

On a good day a wagon train might cover 15 miles. On other days the train hardly moved at all, especially if it had to cross a river. There were no bridges, so the pioneers had to plan how they would get to the other side.

If the river was not too deep, the wagons, people, and animals rolled or walked across as best they could. The things inside the wagon were only a little wet when everyone got to the other side. The people and animals would be wet and muddy, but that was all.

A wagon train crosses a deep river.

If there were heavy spring rains, the rivers would rise. Rivers were harder to cross when the water was deep and fast flowing. Each wagon had to be lifted off its wheels and floated across like a raft or a boat. People on either side tried to guide the wagon with ropes. Animals would swim. Sometimes the rushing water tipped a wagon and people and things fell out and floated away.

There were no roads or even trails over steep mountains. The animals had to pull the wagons to the top. On the way down, ropes were attached to the wagons. People held onto the ropes to keep the wagons from going down too fast. If the ropes broke, a wagon and everything in it would tumble to the bottom of the mountain and be smashed.

When the wagon train finally stopped for the night, there was more work to be done. The wagons were brought together in a circle. The animals were put inside the circle for safety. More water had to be carried. Fires were started for cooking. It was usually the children's job to gather sticks and branches for the fire during the day as they walked.

On the prairie there weren't many trees, so there was little wood to use to make a fire. Then the children had to find something else that would burn. Because there were a lot of buffalo on the prairie, there were a lot of buffalo chips. Buffalo chips were what the pioneers called the pats of buffalo dung, or waste material, that had dried in the strong prairie sun. Buffalo chips made an excellent fire. They burned well with little smell.

Buffalo on the plains

23

Even though life on the trail was hard, it wasn't all work. At night after dinner the pioneers got together for music and games. Men and women brought out fiddles, guitars, and harmonicas. Children sang and danced. On a quiet night, children might play hide and seek in the circle of wagons.

The wagon circle at day's end was a place to relax and to rest. Tomorrow would begin another long day of traveling.

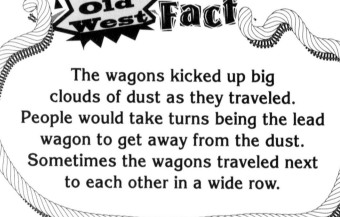

Old West Fact

The wagons kicked up big clouds of dust as they traveled. People would take turns being the lead wagon to get away from the dust. Sometimes the wagons traveled next to each other in a wide row.

Chapter
4 Pioneers and
Native Americans

**A**lthough the pioneers believed they were going into an unknown wilderness, many people lived on the land west of the Missouri River. Native Americans had been living in different tribes in the western part of North America for hundreds of years.

Native Americans traveled the plains following the buffalo.

The tribes spoke different languages and had their own customs. Yet even though the tribes were different from each other and from the pioneers, some things about them were the same. Just like pioneer children, Native American children helped their families with chores. They carried water. They hunted for nuts and berries. They also played many of the same games.

From their parents and grandparents, Native American children learned to hunt, fish, and find wood for fires. Like pioneer children, Native American children also liked to sing songs, tell stories, and dance.

A Kiowa child on a horse

Pioneers and Native Americans meet and trade.

Sometimes the Native Americans helped the pioneers. They gave the pioneers food. They showed them what plants could be eaten. They also helped the pioneers cross rivers and showed them the best routes to take.

As more and more people came to settle in the western lands, trouble began. The Native Americans felt that their lands were being stolen by these new settlers.

There were other problems, too. The Native Americans who lived on the prairie believed the buffalo was a sacred animal. They treated the buffalo with great respect. They hunted them only when they needed food.

No part of the buffalo went to waste. The buffalo's leather hide was used to make clothing, tipis, and even some kinds of canoes. Pieces of buffalo hide that were left over were used to make balls or tiny doll clothes. The buffalo fur was used to make rugs and blankets. The bones were carved into cups and spoons, knives, and arrowheads.

The pioneers had a completely different idea. To them there seemed to be plenty of buffalo. They killed the big animals for meat and for leather and, most upsetting to the tribes who lived on the Plains, simply for sport.

Some Native Americans lived in cone-shaped tents called tipis.

At first the killing of the buffalo worried the Native Americans. They began to wonder how they would be able to live if there were no more buffalo. Then the Native Americans became angry. They could not understand why the pioneers would go on killing this sacred animal until almost none were left.

Some Native Americans began to fight back. They attacked wagon trains. Then the settlers would attack the Native Americans. Often it was hard to tell who started the problem. It wasn't long before the United States Army joined the battle to try to protect the pioneers from attacks. It was a terrible time for both pioneers and Native Americans.

As more pioneers came west and settled on the land, there was less room for the Native Americans. By the late 1840s all of the land the Native Americans lived in had become a part of the United States. The United States government began telling the Native Americans where they could live. Because these places were set aside, or reserved, for the Native Americans, they became known as reservations. Many tribes who had been used to following the buffalo over many miles now had to live in a strange place all year round.

Finally the Native Americans stopped fighting. They knew they couldn't win. As the Native Americans were sent to the reservations, more and more settlers began moving into the lands where the Native Americans had once lived.

Old West Fact

Chief Joseph, a leader of the Nez Perce, always wanted peace. When the U.S. government said he and his people had to leave their lands, some of the warriors fought back. Finally, Chief Joseph surrendered saying, "My heart is sick and sad. From where the sun now stands, I will fight no more forever."

Chapter 5
HOME ON THE RANGE

After a long journey the pioneers finally came to a place they wanted to live. There they started to make a new home.

In the Oregon Territory the pioneers first had to clear the land. They cut down trees to make room for a house, a yard, and perhaps a barn or shed for animals. They also needed fields for planting crops.

An old illustration shows how pioneers lived in their wagons while they built new houses.

Log cabin

Clearing the land was hard work. It took a long time. When enough trees had been cut, the pioneers built log cabins. They chose the longest, straightest logs they could find. Then they made wide cuts in the ends of the huge logs so the logs would fit together. Layers of logs were laid one on top of another to form the sides of the cabin. Cracks were filled with mud and straw. Finally, the pioneers cut timbers to form a roof and covered it with pieces of bark or wooden slats.

After the house was built, a door and some windows would be cut out of the logs. At first, wooden slats were used to cover the windows. Much later the family might get glass window panes. Glass kept out the wind better than wood and also let in light.

Inside of a log cabin

Inside the cabin the floor was made of hard earth. Later the family might put in a floor made from logs that had been cut to make flat boards.

At one end of the log cabin was a fireplace made of stones. There was no electricity at the time of the pioneers. The fireplace served as a furnace for heat, a stove for cooking, and for light. Pioneers also used candles and oil lamps for light. Candles and oil were costly, so they were not used unless it was necessary. The family would try to do everything they could by daylight.

When the sun went down, the family would eat by the light of the fire. Everyone went to bed when it was dark and got up when the sun rose. It was a long day.

On the prairie there were few trees. The pioneers that settled there had to find something other than wood to make houses. They ended up using the ground.

The tough prairie grass had roots that grew together to form a mat of soil. This was called sod. It was so tough even a metal plow had a hard time cutting through it. So the pioneers invented a special plow to cut chunks of sod out of the ground.

These chunks of sod were used just like bricks. The pioneers carefully stacked them one on top of another to build a sod house, leaving spaces for a door and windows. Then they filled any cracks with dirt and mud.

Cutting and loading sod bricks

The people who built the sod houses became known as sodbusters. The pioneers didn't care how unusual their sod homes looked. The important thing was that they had a home.

The thick earthen walls of a sod house kept it warm and cozy in winter, and in summer it was much cooler than a log cabin. The tough dirt bricks were fireproof too, so the pioneers didn't have to worry as much about wind-driven sparks from prairie fires.

When it rained, water often seeped in through the roof. In dry weather, dirt flaked down from the roof, covering everything with a layer of dirt.

A family poses for a picture outside their sod home.

Another kind of sod house was called a dugout. A dugout home was just what the name sounds like. The pioneers would dig a cavelike house out of a hill on the prairie. Then they would use sod to fill in parts of the roof and the front of the house. It looked a little like a cave with a front door and windows added to it.

A dugout sod home

Old West Fact

In time, some people came to love their earthen homes. They put carpets on the dirt floors and colorful cloth on the walls. Even when lumber could be bought for a new home, many people stayed in their "soddies."

6

PIONEER SCHOOLS

hen the pioneers first settled in the West, there were no schools for the children to go to. Many pioneer children were taught to read and write at home by their mothers and fathers. Children didn't have much time for books. They also had to help run their families' farms.

Pioneer children had to know how to start a fire for heat on a freezing cold morning. They learned how to feed the farm animals and how to milk a cow. They learned how to use a plow.

Children help to gather melons with their wagon pulled by turkeys. **37**

Much of the work pioneer children did every day was almost like a lesson. Instead of sitting at a desk and adding numbers, they would be measuring out chicken feed or figuring out how many nails they needed.

Many families earned money by selling whatever they made on their farm. It might have been butter made from the milk they got from their cows, or eggs they gathered from their chickens. It might have been bacon from their pigs, or grain they grew in their fields.

A child of 11 or 12 might have been expected to drive a cart into town, sell the farm goods, and return home with the money while his or her parents worked on the farm. A child also might have been sent into town on horseback to bring back supplies. He or she needed to understand math in order to buy the things the family needed.

A teacher and her students in front of their sod schoolhouse

As more and more pioneers settled in the West, frontier communities grew into small towns. Then several families would get together to build a schoolhouse. The schools were built the same way as houses were, either made of logs or sod.

The families who had children to send to the school would collect money. They would use this money to hire a teacher. Teachers were not easy to find. In some schoolhouses the teachers were not much older than the students. It was not unusual for a boy or girl of 14 or 15 to be teaching school.

Families also agreed to give the teacher a place to live. Some communities built a small house for the teacher. Usually, though, the families would take turns having the teacher stay at their houses.

Because homes were usually far apart, the school wasn't always nearby. Some children had to get up while it was still dark to begin a long walk. Others might have been lucky enough to have their own horses. They could ride to school.

Just as they do now, most children stayed in school all day. They brought their lunch from home in an old tin or pail. Inside there might have been a jar of milk, a piece of cornbread, and an apple.

The potbellied stove kept a one-room schoolhouse warm.

Just like the pioneers' log cabins or sod homes, the frontier schoolhouse was one big room. Also like the cabins, it often had a dirt floor. There was a fireplace or a potbellied stove for heat in the winter. In addition to teaching, it was part of the teacher's job to keep the fire going in cold weather.

The children would have to work on their lessons while the teacher worked with different groups. Ten-year-olds might have been figuring out answers to a math test while the teacher led the five-year-olds in saying the alphabet. The schoolroom could be a very noisy place.

Many children went to school for only a few weeks or months during the year. The rest of the time they had to help their families on the farms. Schooling was something many people prized but few were able to get.

Children helped with farmwork on the prairie.

Old West Fact

The summer vacation that children have today is left over from the time when pioneer children needed to help their families plant and harvest crops in the summer and early fall.

TAKING
A BREAK

Living in the West was hard, but not every minute was spent working. When pioneer children finished everything they had to do, they had the big outdoors to play in. They could race their ponies, walk the hills looking for flowers, swim in a pond, or play with their animals.

Modern children dressed as pioneers show how to play a frontier game.

Community picnic

The most fun for everyone was when a community would get together for a dance or a picnic. People would come from miles around bringing baskets of food. The children played tag, jumped rope, and flew kites. Adults and children joined together to sing songs, play ball games, and run races.

Dances were usually held outside or in the biggest building in town, such as the schoolhouse. Most communities had at least one person who could play a fiddle. The music would start, and people would dance late into the night.

Once in a while traveling entertainers would come through the small western towns. Some of these entertainers were magicians and jugglers. Some groups would put on plays.

In the summer a circus might have come to town. All of the townspeople and the children would come to watch the horses, elephants, and circus performers parade down the streets. Some children would run to the field where the circus was performing and help put up the tents.

A circus parade on the main street of a frontier town

Girls run races on the Fourth of July.

One of the biggest holidays of the year in a frontier town was the Fourth of July. The holiday honored the beginning of the United States as a country.

The morning started with cannon fire. People living far away from town listened for the boom. Then families got into their wagons and rode into town.

As the day went on, people gave speeches. Someone read the Declaration of Independence. Later there might have been a parade.

After a big picnic at noon, people played games, ran races, and joined in pie-eating or pig-catching contests. When the sun finally went down, fireworks were set off.

The children who took part in these celebrations were the children who had traveled across the country to find a new home. Many of them were probably proud of themselves, their families, and their neighbors for living through so many hardships.

Soon the children in these early towns grew up. Then they had children of their own. As more people moved in, the Old West settled down. By the end of the 1800s, the move westward was nearly over.

A pioneer girl

Old West Fact

Many people in frontier towns loved to go to plays. They would shout warnings and cheer on the actors. Some theatergoers knew the plays by heart and would call out the words when an actor forgot them.

GLOSSARY

canvas (KAN vus) a strong, heavy cloth made of cotton

celebrations (seh luh BRAY shunz) events to honor special days, such as holidays

community (kah MYOO nuh tee) all the people who live and work in a place

customs (KUS tumz) ways of doing things used by a group of people for a long time

fertile (FIHR tul) able to produce large crops

frontier (frun TIHR) the border between a settled area and an unsettled area

sacred (SAY krud) given or having the right to great honor; set apart for a spiritual reason

territory (TER uh tor ee) a large stretch of land ruled by a nation or state

tribes (trybz) groups of people or families living together under a leader or a chief

utensils (yoo TEN sulz) tools used for a special purpose, such as cooking